IE807467

A Love Tap

poems

Bernardo Wade

lookout
LOOKOUT BOOKS
University of North Carolina Wilmington

©2025 by Bernardo Wade

All rights reserved. No material in this book may be copied or reproduced in any form or by any electronic or mechanical means, including information storage-and-retrieval systems, without the express written consent of the publisher, except for brief quotations in critical articles and reviews.

First printing, October 2025
ISBN: 9781940596587

Cover design by Emily Louise Smith
Cover art: "I Want My Spot Back" © Abdi Farah
Interior design by Nicole Callahan, Yazmin Flores, and Felicia Rosemary Urso
Author photo © Liza Voloshin

Library of Congress Control Number: 2025942251

LOOKOUT BOOKS
Department of Creative Writing
University of North Carolina Wilmington
601 S. College Road
Wilmington, NC 28403
lookout.org

to the Wades

I can't read minds,
but I can read mine.

—Pops

CONTENTS

FOREWORD
by Ross Gay

The poet Gerald Stern says, "There's something called 'working your way into a poet's mind,'" by which I think he means there's something called working your way into a poet's *heart*, where we can consider not only what the poems do, or how, but maybe also why. In some cases, as W. H. Auden might have put it, what hurt the poems were birthed of. In others, what magic, what sweetness, what gathering of angels. What music, what memory. What confusion. What confession. What deflection, or genuflection. Or, as Yusef Komunyakaa writes it, what need: *the need gotta be / so deep words can't / answer simple questions.*

The first word of Bernardo Wade's *A Love Tap* is "sober," which gives perhaps an unsubtle hint to some of the deep need this book comes out of. Comes through and turns over. Some need to confront and reconcile with a former self—former selves—or come to terms with, or understand, or forgive even, and mourn. In the poem "The Hymn," Wade writes, "Tonight, the boy / you've already grieved crawls / through the window / of who you once were / & whispers, / *Listen. Listen.*" Grieving is a need, whether we cop to it or not, and it's one of these poems' most florid needs, their needs most bountiful and deep. Sometimes the grief hits like the turn in a Richard Pryor monologue or a Dickinson half-rhyme. Like a two-by-four I mean; it is devastating I mean. It hits, it abides, like a stranger covering your body with his coat on a jailhouse floor I mean. Or, like the old counselor who puts his hand so gently on your shoulder that "... tears—real ones—fall / not to the floor / but deep inside someone desperate / enough to live." *The need gotta be / so deep....*

Lest I be making these poems sound heavy-handed or overwrought, they're not. In fact, one of the pleasures of Wade's poems is that they shirk neither humor nor swagger nor play nor a little not-quite-subtle shit talk. (Full disclosure: I have played hundreds of hours of one-on-one with Wade—who in non-book-introduction life I call "B," or other things—and have been the recipient and admirer and sometimes rebuker of said shit talk.) These poems, even when they're hurting, enjoy themselves. They flash a smile at you time to time. They're stylish. They're interested in the tilt of their cap, the cuff of their jeans; not only what the words mean, but how they lean, how they sound. They want to be pretty on their way to being beautiful. On their way to being true. That's need too. It's a kind of tender bravado that reminds me sometimes of Etheridge Knight. And Richard Pryor. And some of our beautiful falsetto singers, maybe Ronald Isley or Moses Sumney. But Wade's falsetto has a little sand in it.

And this tender bravado is most evidenced in the poems about his relationship to his father, to which I find myself—maybe for my own Daddy reasons, definitely because they're beautiful—returning again and again. Though Wade writes about all kinds of relationships—to New Orleans, to lovers and friends, to his mother—it's his father he most returns to, probably because it's the most vexing of those relationships. And so often it's what vexes us; it's the vexing that makes poems come and makes poems go. It's what we don't know. Those poems feel like they need to find another register or dip into another well. They are some of the more mysterious poems in the book, as in the final poem, when the child version of the speaker cries "not tears, but the butterflies / his stomach spills / from his eyes." And in the poems I return to most, "dear fox" and "the coming of fox." The stories, what we've been told, what we've inherited, what we've been given, are illuminated, and transformed, by what is unknowable. In these cases, visitation by foxes who are, or at least invoke, the poet's father and his grandmother. These poems shimmer in strange and yearning light. It's beautiful and apt that Wade's fox poems are after Lucille Clifton's—of course they are—for who better to help us attend to the unknowable. To help us regard what we cannot understand. Which maybe is why we come to poems in the first place. And maybe why poetry comes to us.

I could go on admiring these poems, and I could go on wondering about them—how they flirt with the soil, the trees, the garden; their dalliance with music, and how they dance; their poetic ancestry; the questions they make me ask about love and family, about memory and repair—but nothing I can say will be more compelling to you than Bernardo Wade's poems.

Faith or another way of being

sober. My imagination—still picking at wounds—spots in the Sunday second line my father dressed like a perfect poorboy with hot sauce, bereft of bank-teller pleasantries. He needs napkins. He drips on the scene. Tell him I forgive the generation that moonwalked across the yellow brick road. I found the Tin Man humming "A Few of My Favorite Things" at the daiquiri shop. A man with no heart must find another's drum to beat. Kendrick Lamar says we got daddy issues. But it's on me. Sometimes, it's the fear of falling asleep. A child holds a match to the gasoline of my dreams. He's in my feelings. You ever negotiate with an apparition? *Putting a thing to rest is not a sign of defeat.* My father's epistemology for *motherfucker*, for *drunk*, for *junkie* I make holy with a rosary strung together with Mardi Gras beads. I ask God to *throw me something, Mister*. By *something*, I mean mercy.

i.

Shake Loose the Tree

My mother, wearied by knuckling on & on
into tough dough, used to negotiate with the pilot

light like the rent depended on it. Because it did.
Because the work had to be done that night

I knew to pour her glass red & to handle *Baduizm*
with soft fingers. Eleven & listening & peeling shrimp

& feeling the walls pulse against ain't-shit men,
unaware this was her way of saying, please

don't be like them. "You better call Tyrone" wasn't my jam
but my mother knew every word, she knew

when I returned at dawn, fourteen & still high
on my growth spurt, there weren't enough *I'm sorrys*

in the world to change her mind. *You better call*
your father wasn't a song I'd heard before

but I knew it was mine. It was the first time I said *fine*
when I meant, please…I'll do anything…

while the woman in front of me just stared, knowing
how fruit rots once it falls from the tree.

Super Bowl LIV

I don't feel nervous
but my left leg
jackhammers the floor,
& of course he says,
Boy, you & that fucking leg
in a way most decent folk
might clock as violent,
though this is our way
of seeing one another.
We meet for a sport
more ancestral than football;
call it *don't flinch.*
Halfway through an exhale
my pops ashes his joint.

motherfuckers…
me & Olin, we used to sell
cold drinks & shit for the Saints
games, you know, when they
was at Tulane Stadium. No nets
behind the goal, so after the kicks
people'd be fighting over the ball.
One time, after an extra point,
Olin jumped all the way up
& snatched that ball like a god,
smiling all the way down. But them,
they took that ball. They was men.
We… we was just boys.

& then they was them: white men
& women losing their minds
on national television
over a Patrick Mahomes
touchdown in the last seconds
of a thrilling-ass game

& we were silent.

Another (Damn) Crow Poem

Once the leaves abandon the tree,
the crows, who seem to sense
the loneliness of a limb,
rise up like musical notes
syncopated to the brisk
winter wind. In one swift
descent, the roost glides
down with such rhythm,
the elm welcomes them
with the outstretched arms
of an old, familiar friend.
I watch them huddle close
like strange fruit nestling
for warmth—the survival of kin.
People give crows a bad rap.
I bet none of them get to be young
& foolish, because no one
imagines tenderness from feathers
so black. I wonder if the mother
crow sits her chicks down to impart
the resilience behind black wings,
preening ancestral wisdom
with the most gentle pecks:
kisses that say *I love you, I love you*
when the world won't & thinks
you're a myth or a bad omen
or names a murder
after you & your friends.

This Shit Is Not Interesting

This is what I know about memory—
            it flickers when it feels
like it. & right now it lights
            every corner of the night

Nick & I got twisted off daiquiris.
            He had a toothy smile.
He's gone—a story for another time.
            I still wish I'd stayed

with him for another drink,
            but, running late to meet Slim,
I felt those achy chills creeping
            down the back alley

of my neck. Here, I want you
            to remember Richard Pryor's
Live on the Sunset Strip—his show after
            he smoked himself on fire,

you know, where he lights a match
            & says, "What is that?…
Richard Pryor running down the street!"
            & like smoke, the crowd

rises to their feet. It only takes
            the price of admission to see
your boogeyman drown
            in the ugliest of his defeats.

I know, this shit is not interesting
            to the ones who knew, offstage,
Rich so often slipped away
            into spells of *God, not again.*

& I, who disappeared that week,
    finally saw her text & flew
across town because I knew
    this time she was serious:

She'd thrown my shit—
    all of it—behind the dumpster.
Hold on, let's say a prayer
    for the brothers who don't

make it. God, bless the hot-blooded men
    who find blue lights
knifing through the night.
    Amen to those who bare

teeth, who fight. Thus, when I turned onto
    Dorgenois Street, down
the same one-way where nine years later
    I mourned a beloved killed

by a drunk driver—a driver who could
    have been me—I saw those lights
& thought to run, but then
    thought *hell nah* & pulled over.

I took the stage. Knew it was my time
    to boogeyman into
the light. So I lifted my hands
    just right, fingers spread so wide

you might have thought I was aflame.
    Pryor does say, "That fire
will sober your ass up quick."
    With the amount of dope

tucked away in my draws,
    I thought to swallow it,

but there he was, his Glock already
in my face. He said,

Don't you...fucking...move.
When they tackled my ass
both my tennies flew away.
Fuck fell from my lips

when 12 found enough for a bid
in my waist. He smiled
& I swear I heard a round of applause.
Like Pryor, I was a puddle

of sweat when I walked offstage
& read RESISTING ARREST
on those multicolored sheets.
After a few hours of peacocking,

my stomach tangled itself,
clamoring *more please more*
until the ache for death
knelt me down near a man

who complained a half hour
about his baby mama's expired tags
before he saw the animal writhing.
I lay so childlike, I could almost taste

my mother's gumbo on Christmas Day,
or how a soft blanket might feel
against my skin. I know, I know
this shit is not interesting

unless you know the warmth
that comes once a stranger
takes his coat & covers your body
on a jailhouse floor.

dear fox

after Lucille Clifton

this morning
I found a mess

of your small prints
scattered

across this fresh layer
of frost

now ugly
with the unforgivable light

of another day
where you sister fox

hide somewhere
beyond the lawn

strutting
in your flag of fur

the way
my grandmother

Ms Cleo does
in the dream where her son

fresh off his "vacation"
asks her

why God abandoned him
again

& again I imagine his
question

to be so damn
foolish

because what spoiled him
wasn't her hand

guiding his
as is our family's myth

it's the legend
she's never left us

that for some reason
when jailed

& brought
before my own wounds

my first prayer
asked for the help of his

dead mother
whom I've never seen

or heard or smelled
or touched

but knew
her habit wasn't to hide

like a god
or like you sister fox

she arrived
as she does now

to clown this elegy
to say

chile I’ve done
my work

now let me walk away

The stain

reminds me to slow down, to grip
the wheel with two hands, to glance behind me
endlessly, to remember that the moonlit road slicing
through the limestone ridge is a shadow

slit by my headlights. The rearview mirror
reflects nothing. People say, "Leave the past
behind you," but for Rayshard Brooks,
who just last night, not 100 miles from here,

fell asleep behind the wheel, idling
in a drive-thru, the past *is where he lives.*
How should I look him in the eye when I know
he shouldn't be here, sitting in the back seat,

telling me to bust a U-ey at the storage facility
with the confederate flag, telling me he wants to see
the flames dance all over that Wendy's, then he wants
to go home. God dammit. Is it possible to not be scared

of the dark? Can we pretend he wasn't left
broken over the knee of last night?
In Georgia the mountains rise like fists
trading blows with the bright parts of the sky—

how does his silence whisper itself alive?
"It's only barbeque sauce on your sleeve," he says.
"Give that pedal some gas, let's pretend nothing is
chasing us. Let's go find nowhere to rest."

My Pops Says He Wants His Popeyes Hot

I pass the parking lot
of the Monteleone
where Shorty
valets cars

& tonight
I throw him
a half-hearted salute
like, *I'll catch up with you…*

but really
I'm dodging him
after last week
when he confessed
his fetish for pregnant women
forgetting my sister
sat listening
from the backseat

& though she rolled her eyes
& said, *gross…*

the image of Shorty & whoever's lady
is on my mind
as he tosses a pair of keys
to Mr Steve
the bank teller
down at the Whitney
who gives me ugly looks
& whines about losing his job
& then about his boyfriend
before he cashes
the check

which is a game we play
all of us
complicit in trying

to make things work with
what's not there
until it is, thank God,

so I can make my way
toward Canal
down this dark-ass alley
to get his dinner
which I don't mind
except, sometimes, the Quarter
can get foul

like last Carnival
just over there—in the shadows
of that dumpster
I saw a man playing
with himself
& when he looked over his shoulder
right at me
hopeful I might offer him
the satisfaction
of a soft eye

I did how I was taught—
I didn't look down
or too up
but straight like a man
with no question mark
in his mouth
I stayed cool, I kept saying,
Just stay cool

muscling through my urge to flee
I crossed the alley
knowing if he followed me
I'd be ready

& just the thought of this
makes this street
so alive
with his ghost
I barely notice the scene
growing thick
outside the Burger King

where a boy opens the side door
& the sound of screams
follows him
as he stumbles out
with a cornered animal

growing wild in his eyes
searching everywhere
just before
they find mine

& fuck, do I want to run
when I notice his belly bleeding
but he's locked in
& now I'm holding my arms out

because he's pried open
the part of me my pops calls
my sweet side
that won't deny his weight
falling into mine
as we both hit the ground
& then he's reaching for something
I believe only he & I can see

because for a moment
the alley goes bright
with what looks like great wings

& I think yes, it's just a dream!
but no, it's NOPD
whipping their lights up the wall
swarming the scene
& within moments the boy's gone

& I blink
& then somehow
I'm waiting in line
at Popeyes at the same time
I do most nights

thinking, dang Shy is on fry
I forgot to change
clothes

then I hear, *Look!*
Catholic boy here!
Five minutes on the chicken!
Tell ya pops it's gon be hot tonight!

& the other workers smile
as he makes
prayer hands
then points to my shirt—
its khaki fit
part of a Jesuit uniform
uncommon for the midnight shift—

he says, *Nigga, is that blood on your shirt?*

& before I can even respond
he's distracted
by a group of girls just stumbling in
carrying those grenades
that smell like the sewers
on Bourbon.

Portrait of a Black Walnut Tree

Mr. George, a surly old man
we moved next door to after the divorce,

slid me a few dollars one afternoon
along with a note that read,

Love your mother, do good by her &, I swear,
it was the very next day

he raised his cane to the sky & hailed me over
like he was rounding up a flock of pigeons

or maybe he was poking at God
to bless us, in New Orleans, with a lil rain.

The weather man warned us that day
to stay inside—with the funky-ass window units

we never turned on—so I was thinking,
this fool wants to meet his maker

as he shuffled into his furnace of a shed
past sixty years of rusted golf clubs, yard signs, & old tools

just to pull out this ancient mower
that wouldn't start till he seduced it with a few sonofabitches,

some WD-40, & all the strength my twelve-year-old bicep
could muster against a motor

caked in years of rust & muck.
He was such a hard-ass that, just like he told me

to keep away from Junie & Peanut
my partners in wheelies & double dutch & tag,

he would sit there & make sure
I mowed his lawn's stripes—straight

& careful—as I still do today in Bloomington,
where this huge black walnut tree

leaves so many fragrant
tennis-ball-sized fruit hiding in the tall grass.

I started whining about them
at a potluck in this crunchy town obsessed

with its trees, &, of course, some dude explains
that when my mower bazookas

the walnut brains across the lawn,
I'm spreading this toxin

that creates a kind of territory around its neighbors,
which, on the surface, makes it a menace

unless you're of a species
that somehow sways this toxin to protect you

& your family.

It's Hard for Me to Tell You This Without Picturing It

I wish I could forget the night I snuck into my parents' room,
testing the door, lightly jostling it, until I wedged myself
through a crevice & then crept in with the same soft steps my auntie,
usually a little tipsy, liked to warn me about, saying, *Don't trust men*
who don't finish their plate or can't be heard when they walk
through your home. Mind you I wasn't a man, but a boy who fledged his way
onto the mattress's corner. Nestled between wanting to be held & playing
possum, I heard my mother's breath begin to escalate to a sound
I associated with Marilyn Monroe, our cocker spaniel,
who'd sometimes whimper from delight, begging for another treat.
Then my father began to speak, & his low, sweet tone surprised me;
he sounded like a child, working his wants out. He said, *Yes baby yes*
then I said *What baby?*... & my mother fell off the bed screaming, so I laughed
just like you might have, just now, & he said *This motherfucker* & laughed back.

ii.

Listening to Nigel Hall Cover "Golden Time of Day" at Lafayette Square

A butterfly blows bubbles
over the crowd—this the Big Easy.

Her purple Vans loosening
their tongues, each step in rhythm.

Nigel is off-key, like this poem,
& it's beautiful

how the butterfly's partner has a picture
frame around his neck—

we are emerging from his imagination.
The four horsemen hold up

their squad car. Unfortunately,
they are beautiful too.

One officer, palms swaying with the sky,
looks above & offers his heart.

So I join him,
but I'm not really seeing the light

of Heaven or some other metaphor
to save what's broken.

No, my mother emerges from the glow
of my imagination.

She holds a glass of wine
& weighs the possibility of rain.

She says, I'm not here to be
your little muse—you can

save all those tears.
Can't you see it's shining!

A Woman and a Child in the Doorway, Harlem, 1975

after a photograph by Dawoud Bey

Don't look into the eyes
        of that baby for too long—
she's made of mirrors.
        Last week, she blinked

& left a chatty couple tongueless.
        She spoke ill of
their silence. Told me shadows
        like to run off

& then asked me to play.
        Don't listen to her mama
if she says, *C'mon, don't be scared…*
        Notice her right foot,

halfway shadow & halfway
        light, ready to stomp
someone beneath its sole—
        maybe where they believe

you belong. Hold on. We know Death
        isn't some dark tunnel,
& the lightbulb at the end
        of this hallway isn't a metaphor

for heaven, so let's start over.
        Look into her eyes, now breathe
as she stares into that place
        within you & asks, *Do I disappear*

when you close your eyes? Her mama
        pulls her up higher, then curls
her little fingers even closer
        because she must. Because you

won't…People say God is light—
maybe that's how the baby sees it;
she points us to the image
& says, *That little piece of bright is ours.*

Before She Blooms

Not long after the fight,
my ex biked over

& murdered our plants,
leaving them in little explosions

of terra-cotta & soil.
When I found the maypop,

the spiderwort, the bird of paradise,
& all the others

I was learning to care for,
I was confused because she

had loved them
like children.

Only the wisteria—burrowed deep,
with its poisonous leaves

& sturdy neck—
withstood the kind of rage

no person plans.
It was me—not the plants—

she wanted   to hurt
to leave

feeling something   horrible
like how she felt—

she later confessed.
But it takes a special devotion to rid oneself

of an invasive species
that speaks in *I'm sorrys.*

Weeks later,
after another drunken disaster

where Fat Tuesday
became a siege

over the front door, I woke up
on the porch

& found her outside watering the wisteria.
Might be another year

before she blooms, she said
like she knew

she'd kick rocks
before its purple flowers bruised the sky,

the house finally strangled
by its vine.

Delirium Has His Way

I'm halfway down the stone stairs
flat on my back
when I realize I'm so fucking in love
my bruised tailbone
doesn't matter, it doesn't matter
I've blown half my savings
on a four-day trip to Paris
with a stranger
who says she ain't ready
to commit. Tonight,
Delirium tastes of pâté
& cheap burgundy
& I don't know much French
but the slimy way he repeats
s'il vous plaît, s'il vous plaît, s'il vous plaît,
with his hands all over me
makes me believe I'm a beautiful scene—
cherry blossoms raging
into the Seine or a storm
kissing Sacré-Coeur—
I'm nothing but a loverboy
crooning after a dream.
But some dreams have braces,
drive a Mazda 626
& make me say it, *I love you,*
every time I get off the phone
& I really feel
like, maybe, someone
out there is finally mine
& Delirium shows me our kids
& the house we would raise them in
& my perfect job
& I think, damn, that was easy
but then one day
my dream tells me
she doesn't believe in dinosaurs
& thinks the earth is flat
& Delirium shifts the whole fucking world
just like that.

God Made Dirt, & Dirt Ain't Popeyes

a sestina broken to bits

I'm one parable short of grasping how someone
dipped that first thigh in the perfectly
churned milk, which may have tasted
a little sour, like childhood. Or, like
a yearning to crawl back inside
a simpler time: We'd pray my mother, down

in her purse, had enough coin to throw down
on a Big Box. Doesn't hunger begin with someone's
mother, nestling them just inside
her hip's curve as she wraps them perfectly
down her back, enclosing the space, holding them like
I'll never let you go—now taste

the body's work. & what a child tastes
of their own genesis goes down
gently, as I taste this chicken today, like
Dang, what is buttermilk? Give someone
enough hunger & they'll discover all the perfect
ways to use the milk inside

another animal. I eat the biscuits inside
my car because I can't wait to taste
my last dollar. My mother put it perfectly:
Slap him 'cause my hand hurts. Don't ask how we survive down
in New Orleans, a city where someone
simmers the cayenne-soaked grease bucket like

God lit the fire because He felt a mother's pressure, like
he wanted a day off from feeding these children.

Mountain Baptism

for L

you led me to a wood
so slick with mud
I didn't make it a hundred feet
before you noticed
my face twist
toward my Nike Dunks,
then, like a mother
might nudge a child
into a school's gate,
I felt you, oh so gently,
touch me
on the meat of my left arm
right above the elbow,
not saying a word,
which was probably smart,
as I'm known to argue
about the gall of white folks
leading other folks
on "adventures"
their Black friends
might suck their teeth at,
might say something like,
"could neva" or,
more specifically,
as one of my friends
actually said,
responding to a pic
from this very trip,
"your white side is showing."
& I bit my tongue,
so to speak,
braving the snowy mud
as I followed you on our ascent
which was a nice view
of your hiking boots

showing off
with each step
the ease at which
you could outpace me,
& I chalked it up,
because I'm prideful,
to your lifetime
of weaving
through these white aspens
that I can tell you love
as you keep pointing to their crowns,
likening their new leaves
to a woman's lashes.
& when we reached
the trail's clearing
you looked back
& I got it,
the earth revealed its shoulders
& it felt like a god
came down,
careless & gifted,
dragging their fingers
across the sky
with the imagination
one finds
tacked to a preschool wall,
while the sun
soaked our limbs
warm, I,
still cautious, wonder
why you turned
down what
I would never consider
a trail, but I followed,
trying to be peaceful,
trying to forget
about the boys

you jokingly called
Hitler Youth
as they tailed our car
with their dog
& four-wheeler
down a road named
Oh Be Joyful.
& I could hardly catch my breath,
thankful you stopped
next to a river
that had a lot
to say,
its current,
a roaring contralto,
reminded me
of the bridge
from Mahalia Jackson's
rendition of
"How I Got Over"
with the occasional
branch snapping
like a handclap
from a Baptist choir
& I asked you,
as you took off
your shoes & socks,
if you were getting in,
imagining how
if that current took you away
I couldn't save you
& I'd have much to explain
to whatever authority
questioned me
about foul play,
but you assured me
you'd be okay,
you'd done this before,

you called it
a Mountain Baptism,
slowly slipping
your feet in the water
& patiently
I sat like a father,
worried his daughter
had messed around
& joined a cult,
paying homage
to some snow god
that promises
an abundance of fresh powder,
knowing for me
this might have meant
cocaine
though for you
it meant winter had
been fruitful
but we were on the back side
of May
so the water you're in
was snow just
minutes ago
& you gave me a look
that somehow
seduced me
to bare feet.
Before I knew it
my toes were in
& you're filming me
saying,
"Oh my God,
that's miserable"
& you're impressed
I think
more with yourself

because despite
the voices
from my childhood
telling me
I'm going
to catch cold,
I'm not mad
or scared,
I'm smiling.

Her Little Laugh

for my friend Ross & his friend Aisha

Though I didn't know her,
that's how it felt—
my friend's silence
so sudden in its effect I play it careful
like *The Shadow of Your Smile*
by Dexter Gordon.
Tangled in his brow,
he stares into an evening
kneeling its light
in a new emptiness.
He says, she had this little laugh…
& though we're still
on the back porch
I can smell the curry wafting
out the kitchen
from the Trini joint in Flatbush,
then somebody's—probably,
everybody's—song comes on,
a glass of water spills
laughter onto the grime-slicked floor
& now it's a party
because she's embarrassed
by her one friend who never minds
climbing atop the table
though soon enough they're both
singing from the deep parts
of themselves, then he pauses
as if someone's there,
he points to a hummingbird,
&, again, we're crowded
by what's in front of us,
his garden, tall with sunflowers,
their heads heavy as the day's end.

iii.

The Hymn

after Marie Howe

Tonight, the boy
you've already grieved crawls
through the window
of who you once were
& whispers,
Listen. Listen.
Thirty days off heroin & he's still here.
You say no—not
again—so it feels like a dream
against your will
holds the flame
under the spoon
& pulls closer your last breath. A sweet
sweet hum begins as the boy stops
the constellation bleeding from the pale crook
of your arm with a kiss,
knowing you would oblige *this*
oblivion *this* strange song
growing loud & lovely louder & lovelier
till you're nothing
but the warmth
of life's slippery *goodnight*
hovering above yourself
you find the boy splashing
through puddles.
It's charming the way he calls to
his dead—
Again! he says, taking your hand,
Don't you want to play…

Ten Minutes Before They Released Me from Orleans Parish Prison

I was moved
to a holding cell
beyond the racket

of the other cages
where a man
rock-bottom with the floor

sat working his tongue,
moving the blood from his lip
down his throat.

His eyes seemed to crawl
toward a kind
of mercy in the wall.

But it was
the latex gloves tied
& filled with days of his waste

that sank
my head into my hands
for our mothers

who'd cared for us
& our stench
this way.

She'd have held him,
but I couldn't
stomach much more

than the cruelty of looking
away—ashamed
that we, broken but still our own,

were desperate
for what I believed decent,
to be left alone.

In the Wake of Ida

When my father calls, I tell him
the damage, how the bricks—
so many of them now
in the street—lie prostrate,

faithful to the earth again.
How Ida darkened the sky,
throwing light at our feet
like doubloons

until she swept the city
beneath her eye—trapping us
like the tree limb
that fell through the window

into the kitchen. He pines.
I know he'll take this
as a sign. Now in L.A.,
he says "Look at God!"

like a man spared. I want
to say, look—you are gray,
the world is drowning,
& I am afraid. Can't you see

these ruins? Your mistakes?
Instead, I say "I love you"
& notice the dawn's first light
breaks with such innocence.

This is the real madness
with a hurricane—the next day
the sun comes out like a parent,
like nothing ever happened.

Origin of a Big Chief

Juju, stumbling out another moon-
shined morning at Teddy's,
saw that first splash of dawn
kiss the shotguns on Prieur
& thought *Damn, now that's pretty!*

Just hours earlier, having felt
all his will cripple
before the old mantra
of *Baby, just one more…*
he knew, at his third whiskey,
there wasn't no fucking
way he'd lift a finger
in any yard the next day.

Besides, he couldn't stand
those pearly-toothed mansions
up near the river,
with their know-nothing owners
always fighting with beauty,
making folk—like him—
strangle it from earth.

Juju felt his hands & thought,
with all that money you'd think
they wouldn't spend it
making everything so
prim so absent so ugly.

But, he knew of their secrets.
Knew for Carnival,
when they paraded downtown
in their white capes & frail gowns,
a good mess of them left
their skins & turned monstrous,

slithering into a vile
corner of the swamp,
lusting after flesh

or, at least, that's the story
Uncle Dunc told
every Ash Wednesday, still high
on the champagne
he swore tasted like lips,
he'd strip his tux
right there on Bienville—flexing,
but not without
the ugly terror
common in the eyes
of men who'd spend Mardi Gras
hustling after snakes
in that way.

Whenever the morning
returned all those beautiful men
to the servile look
of trying to make a way,
Juju joined them, sometimes
crossing the oak-lined avenues
for the kind of work
that felt so foul his bones
went cold & ached.
To remedy, he'd been taught
by his grandmother TeTe
to take a handful of Itla-okla
& think of all the softness
the little moss's life
had collected from the wind.
He'd feel the warmth
of her words & remember
what was theirs—
that their blood was ancient,

that if ever afraid
to remember how deep
in the eyes of their kin,
they could find the prettiest of men
dancing to the beat
of a mighty drum,
their faces lit by a light
that burns in everything,
even in the mosquitos
he felt sucking
his ankles dry. It was a sign
sleep was calling him.

But as he made his way,
Black—a bonafide booster
whose past for doing folk ill,
by then, was mostly forgiven—
appeared like an apparition.
He slung an arm around
Juju's neck, talking so close
the air between them
grew warm with whiskey
& torch fuel on his breath.
He asked, *Love, how come*
you ain't a flambeaux man?

& Juju shrugged, knowing
Black's gold-plated pride
meant the hand working
Juju's pocket wasn't desperate.
Maybe he couldn't help it.

Everybody knew if a man
learned to twirl & strut
& pick up the quick coin
thrown at his feet,
he made out decent, that is

if the dandelion crowd
ponied up that week.
Juju noticed the cooked flesh
festering on Black's arm
& remembered how, as a child,
after he first watched
light leap at the mercy
of their muscles, the fantasy
of parading through
the city bathed in light
carried him home
till his father, a man who'd escaped
to the swamp far before
their war, saw his boy
beginning to twirl & grabbed him
by the eyes & said,
Ain't no fucking son of mine
gonna ever hold a flambeaux!

Then he shuffled off
in one of his fits,
disappearing back into the sky
of his mind, mumbling
as he massaged the scar
running down his neck.
He told Juju to stop working
his nerves, to get gone
so he could sit awhile
with a little wine
&, as he put it,
finally get some damn rest.

Requiem for Guy

After Katrina, we broke
into a FEMA trailer, a haven
filled with burn holes scattered
like little graves. I watched you
wrestle the TV antennae, smiling
because for at least a few hours,
we summoned the soft hum
that sweet-talks bravado off
the brow, sedating our baby-faced
resentments with one another.
What did we know of friendship
but its malice? Once a week
we robbed the first to fall asleep,
reprieved, inevitably, by the need
to forgive the other's suffering.
This kind of love persists,
watching a man drift from life
into its seam, choking down breath,
maybe in a dream where junkies dance
on a blank slate. We were joyful
when you'd get a call, hopping in
your girlfriend's car to go somewhere
else & smoke cigarettes till
we had more small pills staring
back from our palms. Today,
one of my students told me,
You're my guy, but I thought of you
& how many sticky afternoons
we tried to forget our names, handing
them back to God so we could
rest. When I got the call, I knew
He had refused to give yours back.

The Angel of Farewell

after John Keene

I wake to winter's reply—
in mid gait, the snow, as it falls, shapes

this silence & I'm afraid,
again, of the angel grinding her teeth

on empty bottles,
covering the dead grass, shimmering

the earth with what
I can't say: We were young & newly naked,

mangled in precarity,
that Paris room reeked of love—like spring

dew, so I wrote a poem
about the eagerness of May—an elegy for naivety,

now tucked away.
Remember? I used words like *perfect* & *fate.*

But now I lie next to you
mouthing the words *I'm sorry*

across my cold lips,
listening to a stack of plates tremble

inside your breath.

Mercy, Mercy, Mercy

Sometimes we're not prepared for adversity
—CANNONBALL ADDERLEY

Before the barstool,
toes dangled with sweet
inhibition. Don't mind me.
Blow the dust off
the seat. Look
how the roof leaks
moonlight, how flowers
sprout from the mouth
when you speak.
It'll teach you to choke
down beauty & be
discreet. Don't tell Daddy,
says Judas, sucking ice.
He laughs when the cat
walks his horn back—
to forgive is to retreat.
He's got a god up his sleeve.
The blood of a thousand
juke joints flow
into one glass &
he swallows it neat.
Don't believe his rumors.
This is how the missionary
lost his religion—
a cannonball fell
out the rock-bottom sky.
When it landed,
the night knelt
& from its knees
it said,
Mercy, mercy, mercy.

God, please tell him leave

that liquor alone—a prayer
sweat through his paper-bag
skin. I'd sit on his thigh
just to watch him

turn a whole bottle to the sky,
swallow it down
& breathe, happy to breathe.
He'd say, *This here's my medicine*

& I'd smile, knowing his need.
Most days we'd watch
the hood turn colors,
shift shadows till dusk

shrouded us in Blues.
Like a griot, he'd belly up to the keys
& say, *Hear that? That's your people*
spilling across the night's muddy knees.

Said his music was bamboula
& crow & sugarcane & an ocean
of field sweat, conjuring
one question: Why aren't my loves unchained?

Said he wasn't thirsty
for salvation. Shit, swore Jesus Christ
himself hopped down,
left two tears in his bucket & said, *Motherfuck it.*

I still hear his last wish:
One more & I'll smile these golds
before the pearly gates!
In his jazz funeral, I caught

two tears from the sky,
felt he was there, wet my brow
with him. The brass band trilled,
When I die you better second line. Oh Lord,

you better second line & I knew
what made those handkerchiefs strut
like little white doves
drunk on the bass drum's drift.

I remembered
We don't bury our dead
he once said,
'cause our blood is still at play.

iv.

Ars Poetica

In Indiana
pawpaw falls
out the sky;
the path
to their reign
is littered with
lion's mane,
some
chanterelle too.
Calliope—
not the
muse, but my
pup—& I
walk here &
there—a way
to say
we lose track
often—
inside canopies
down paths
that say
CLOSED
'cause we
found God
likes how
accustomed
we are
to the mud
to the way
the rocks feel
wet. & what
if death
hangs like
a gown
counting

the walks
we have
left? It's
in this
dwindled
light
that words fall
from
the trees
like breath.

The Angels of Thirst

i.
It's only noon & the vodka
pouring out Jamal's funk
is more honest
than anything he's admitted

for nine months. He isn't
sober, but every time
I ask, he looks me
dead in the eyes

& says, *yes, king…*
like he's not too distracted
swiping right on all the girls
he'll never meet.

Before he looks up
I'm on him close as a kiss,
lovetappin' his chin—
I think, why are we like this?

Ten years ago I was him,
brushing my teeth in the shower
to avoid the mirror,
coughing up bile each morning,

dying over & over again
as I crawled the mountain
of my thirst, only to find at the summit
some reason to slip back down,

that is, till I slipped into handcuffs
& felt my whole life melt
into *Help… help… I promise God, please…*
I'll do fucking anything…

(but get clean).

ii.
I failed forty-seven drug tests
before the fog lifted
& they ushered me before the choir
of chattering monkeys

they call *rehab*.
Alcohol stilled the voices.
It became your god
& no one can run from a god

said the counselor I gamed to graduate me
—*I know*—a few days early.
An angel of sweet good old boys,
he never skipped chest day

or an opportunity to make one of the guys
from his group tear up
& punch something. His office wall,
a graveyard for fists,

it seemed to tease whoever spoke,
as anger does, & I worried
how many of us, who maybe struck that wall
the way we'd been,

were asking violence to answer
for how it raised us—
graceless & afraid.
Bobbing & weaving his suggestions,

the counselor said many of the wall's holes
honored those
who had already met their end
& that we, no matter our belief,

drank just like them.

iii.
Two weeks in & I found Death
doesn't knock or ring.
He visits in duller moments—
Like I'm singing in the shower

& suddenly *Bam!*, I'm thinking, fuck it
maybe it'll be quick…
Then I can almost see myself lying there
all smiles, dimples stiff

& when I tell this to the counselor
he doesn't flinch or grimace or even sigh
he just points to my heart
& says, *All the shit of your life*

is blocking you from its light.
I tell him I'm through then, that I'll pretend
if that's what it takes
I'll ask whatever fucking god—

the god of doorknobs
the god of toilets
the god of coffee makers
the god of I DON'T CARE

& suddenly, this old geezer
rests his hand
on my shoulder
with so much tenderness

all my stupid pride goes limp
& I feel tears—real ones—fall
not to the floor
but deep inside someone desperate

enough to live.

A Young Man Resting on an Exercise Bike, Amityville, NY, 1988

after a photograph by Dawoud Bey

It's like the young man
readies to spread wings:
elbows splayed on bars,
obsidian shoulders sleek

from the sky's gleam.
His eyes, heavy with quiet
ease, stare into the lens—
a palpable need bites

back a dissenting smile,
muscle memories arrest
his body, filling the scene.
How did Bey ask him

to *act natural*, to pose
all that swagger
for the sufferable
stillness of his small

machine? Captured in
the shadow & the light
is the space between
expression & Black

flight. To pedal nowhere
is to feign the act of flying.
Amityville, a great migration,
so maybe those are wings.

The image is a discourse,
an obliteration of causality.
Notice how his right fist
covets something, forearm

flexed. His left hand
finds the right, fingers
spread calm like whatever
he grips, he'll keep it

quiet as it's kept
from the gaze patrolling
just outside the frame.
He was about to split

but Bey's camera denies
the temporal. The face
of that wristwatch reflects
three hundred years

of waiting on the corner
for nothing to happen.
Bey & the young man survive—
an afternoon, an arm's length.

Tell Him I'm Busy

On a French Quarter sidewalk,
I'm reminded of childhood,
its brevity reflected
in the eyes of this boy—
phone pressed against his ear,
his brow already furled
by a world, which, telling
by his tone, he thinks is real.
His father—in joggers
& Jordans—strolls
up with the swagger
of a broken wing & smiles
like he's proud of the anguish
he's reared. The two
share a moment—pointing
to the phone, the boy rolls
his eyes like, *Can you believe this?*
& my therapist stops me there:
Talk about when your father calls…
Avoidance is a love
language we share.
Do you think you mythologize him?
Sometimes, I imagine him,
pubescent & peach-fuzzed,
bending down to drink
from the BLACKS ONLY fountain,
& then I'm catching his tears
on the day Marvin Gaye's
father reached for a gun.
I know every word to "What's Going On,"
but for some reason
I tell him, *I'm busy,*
I'll call you back when I'm done.

the coming of fox

after Lucille Clifton

now gray
almost like smoke

feeling its way
against the wind

my father glides over
& you let him

steal your bright
flag of fur

to his chest
nuzzling you so close

it almost feels
wrong

watching his knuckles
go soft

without shame
with a love

he's shown me
only once

the night
I pawned his gold ring

& after getting my fix
returned

to his arms
he embraced me

so close
I tasted his wine-breath

& we were no longer
a tangle

of two fiendish men
but became

ugly & tearful
seeing in the other

an animal
neither could hold.

Sleeve of Memory

after Robert Hayden

He taught me no two
smacks are the same.
The ringing still lives in my ear—
a tune dedicated to

be quiet. I swallow his gold ring,
but then cough up
a little boy—his face buried
in his palms, ready to catch

not tears, but the butterflies
his stomach spills
from his eyes. We share these
legs that didn't know

where to run. Neither of us remember
hearing the word *son*
or how to embrace someone in the eyes
when they say, *I love.*

Don't think, *that is such a shame.*
To remember things as they
were is counterintuitive
to survival. I love my father.

See how I did that. I changed
the color of the sky by closing
my eyes to see him at thirteen
scared. If I were anything

like God, I'd hide in the celestial
sleeve of memory & retune the heart-
strings of hard men to offer
them this new language—

where their hands aren't their tool,
but their tongue & then *clap*
like thunder, he'd ask for forgiveness.
Who, God? Yes, him too.

Acknowledgments

My deepest gratitude begins with the literary journal editors who believed my work should be in the world and read by their readers!

Academy of American Poets: "My Pops Says He Wants His Popeyes Hot"
Academy of American Poets *Poem-a-Day* series: "The Hymn"
African American Review: "Origin of a Big Chief"
Beloit Poetry Journal: "Portrait of a Black Walnut Tree"
Black Warrior Review: "A Woman and a Child in the Doorway, Harlem, 1975"
The Cincinnati Review: "This Shit Is Not Interesting" and "Sleeve of Memory"
Crazyhorse: "Another (Damn) Crow Poem," "Shake Loose the Tree," and "A Young Man Resting on an Exercise Bike, Amityville, NY, 1988"
EcoTheo Review: "It's Hard for Me to Tell You This Without Picturing It"
Ecotone: "Requiem for Guy"
Jazz and Culture: "Mercy, Mercy, Mercy"
The Kenyon Review: "Ten Minutes Before They Released Me from Orleans Parish Prison"
The Massachusetts Review: "Her Little Laugh"
Mississippi Review: "Tell Him I'm Busy"
The Nation: "In the Wake of Ida"
Obsidian: Literature & Arts in the African Diaspora: "Listening to Nigel Hall cover 'Golden Time of Day' at Lafayette Square"
Poet Lore: "Before She Blooms"
Poetry Northwest: "Ars Poetica"
Puerto del Sol: "The stain"
The Rumpus: "Delirium Has His Way"
The Sewanee Review: "the coming of fox"
Southern Humanities Review: "God, please tell him leave"
Southern Indiana Review: "The Angel of Farewell"
The Southern Review: "God Made Dirt, & Dirt Ain't Popeyes"
Third Coast: "Faith or another way of being"
West Branch: "Mountain Baptism"

"Requiem for Guy" and "This Shit Is Not Interesting" were reprinted in *Another Last Call: Poems on Addiction and Deliverance*, edited by Kaveh Akbar and Paige Lewis and published by Sarabande Books.

Let me start with how stupefyingly divine an experience I've had working with KaToya and Emily of Lookout Books. These women hold me down.

I wrote and revised many of these poems at institutions that provided me the space, time, and support to do so. Thank you to The Watering Hole Poetry Fellowship, Tin House Workshop, the Mountain Words Writer-in-Residence Program, Indiana University Writers' Conference, the Community of Writers, Sewanee Writers' Conference, Vermont Studio Center, Indiana University's Creative Writing Program, the Stegner Fellowship at Stanford University, and especially the Outpost Residency Program. I am showering praise and thanks on so many folk attached to these institutions—you know who you are—and I pray that you feel the warmth I have for you. Your hearts, minds, and hands made this possible.

These poems have the blessed touch of those gracious enough to weather me bugging them with "Yo, can I read you this real quick?" Shout-out to Gabrielle, El, Joy, Nandi, Steffan, K, janan, Austin, Sarah, Dianelly, Taylor, Dashaun, Cubs, Doug, Matthew, Mercedes, my cohorts at IU and the Stegner, and all of you who listened—or at least humored—my random gall to read to you despite the potentially embarrassing place we were standing or sitting or…you get it. Again, thank you.

A shower of thank yous to all my coaches: Niyi Osundare, Carolyn Hembree, Kalamu ya Salaam, Adrian Matejka, Will Alexander, Duriel E. Harris, Afaa Michael Weaver, L. Lamar Wilson, Terri Simone Francis, Valerie Grim, and of course, the friend I've referred to only as Coach—Rossie.

I'm tremendously grateful to my family: Clee, Mimi, Bayou, Mr. Motherf*cker, Lolo, John, Si, and all the other Wades, Kinbergs, Kings, and Rocketts who make this beautiful life of mine possible.

Lookout is more than a name—it's our publishing philosophy. Housed in the University of North Carolina Wilmington's nationally ranked creative writing department, Lookout Books brings attention to works by emerging and underrepresented writers, as well as overlooked gems by established authors, and offers students apprenticeships in the art and craft of publishing.